ANCIENT CIVILIZATIONS Need to Know

SilverTip

The Rise and Fall of Ancient Greece

by D. R. Faust

Consultant: Caitlin Krieck, Social Studies Teacher and Instructional Coach, The Lab School of Washington

BEARPORT
PUBLISHING

Minneapolis, Minnesot

Credits

Cover and title page, © Rich Lynch/Shutterstock; 4–5, © Stock Montage/Getty Images; 7, © FrankRamspott/iStock; 9, © duncan1890/iStock; 10–11, © IanDagnall Computing/Alamy Stock Photo; 13, © Photo 12/Getty Images; 15, © DEA / ICAS94 /Getty Images; 17, © Anastasios71/Shutterstock; 18–19, © history_docu_photo/Alamy Stock Photo; 21, © Curioso.Photography/Shutterstock; 23, © Ivy Close Images/Alamy Stock Photo; 24–25, © Artepics/Alamy Stock Photo; 27, © Cameron Whitman/Shutterstock; 28a, © duncan1890/iStock; 28b, © Photo 12/Getty Images; 28c, © Curioso.Photography/Shutterstock; 28d, © Artepics/Alamy Stock Photo.

Bearport Publishing Company Product Development Team

President: Jen Jenson; Director of Product Development: Spencer Brinker; Managing Editor: Allison Juda; Associate Editor: Naomi Reich; Associate Editor: Tiana Tran; Art Director: Colin O'Dea; Designer: Kim Jones; Designer: Kayla Eggert; Product Development Assistant: Owen Hamlin

Statement on Usage of Generative Artificial Intelligence

Bearport Publishing remains committed to publishing high-quality nonfiction books. Therefore, we restrict the use of generative AI to ensure accuracy of all text and visual components pertaining to a book's subject. See BearportPublishing.com for details.

Library of Congress Cataloging-in-Publication Data

Names: Faust, Daniel R., author.
Title: The rise and fall of ancient Greece / by D.R. Faust.
Description: Minneapolis, Minnesota : Bearport Publishing Company, [2025] |
   Series: Ancient civilizations : need to know | Silvertip books. |
   Includes bibliographical references and index.
Identifiers: LCCN 2023059641 (print) | LCCN 2023059642 (ebook) | ISBN
   9798892320443 (library binding) | ISBN 9798892325189 (paperback) | ISBN
   9798892321778 (ebook)
Subjects: LCSH: Greece–Civilization–To 146 B.C.–Juvenile literature.
Classification: LCC DF77 .F29 2025 (print) | LCC DF77 (ebook) | DDC
   938–dc23/eng/20240126
LC record available at https://lccn.loc.gov/2023059641
LC ebook record available at https://lccn.loc.gov/2023059642

Copyright © 2025 Bearport Publishing Company. All rights reserved. No part of this publication may be reproduced in whole or in part, stored in any retrieval system, or transmitted in any form or by any means, electronic, mechanical, photocopying, recording, or otherwise, without written permission from the publisher. Bearport Publishing is a division of Chrysalis Education Group.

For more information, write to Bearport Publishing, 5357 Penn Avenue South, Minneapolis, MN 55419.

Contents

What to Watch 4

Shaped by the Land 6

The Rise of City-States 8

Games and Gods 12

Spreading Out 14

Successes and Struggles 16

A Great King 20

An End to It All 22

Gone but Not Forgotten 26

Ancient Greece Timeline 28

SilverTips for Success 29

Glossary 30

Read More 31

Learn More Online 31

Index 32

About the Author 32

What to Watch

Do you like streaming movies or TV? Watching a show has long been a popular pastime. In fact, people were doing it more than 2,000 years ago. Actors performed stories for audiences in ancient Greece. And entertainment isn't the only thing we got from the Greeks!

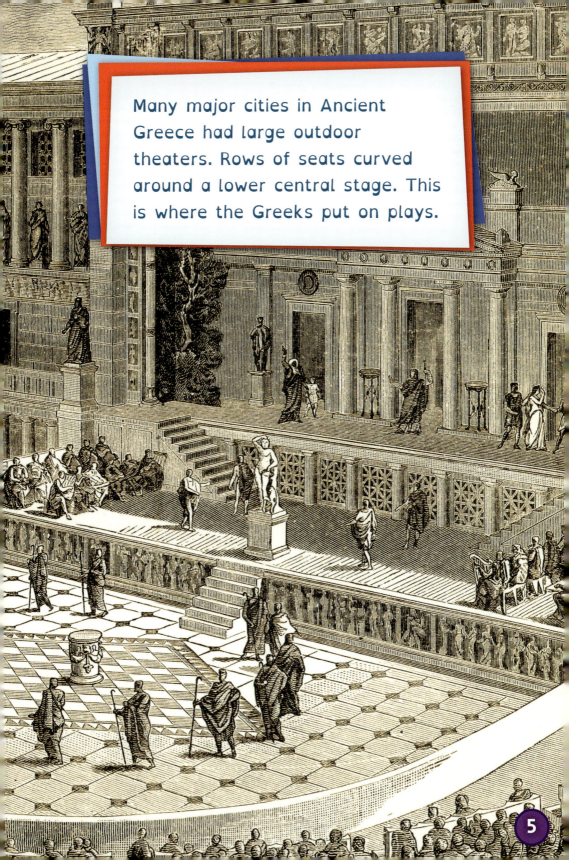

Many major cities in Ancient Greece had large outdoor theaters. Rows of seats curved around a lower central stage. This is where the Greeks put on plays.

Shaped by the Land

Ancient Greece was a land of many mountains. These towering landforms kept people separated. Small groups settled together. They made their homes along rivers and on the coast of the Aegean (i-GEE-uhn) Sea.

Traveling by land was hard. So, the first ancient Greeks used boats to move along these waterways.

The Aegean Sea sits between Europe and Asia. There are more than 1,000 islands in it. The Greeks settled on many of these islands.

The Rise of City-States

As more people gathered in the region, a **civilization** took shape. It began with a time called the Archaic (ahr-KAY-ik) period. This era started as early as 800 BCE. It lasted until 480 BCE.

At first, ancient Greece was not a single, large, powerful region. Instead, it was several strong city-states.

During the Archaic period, Greeks studied science, math, and **philosophy**. The poet Homer wrote the *Iliad* and the *Odyssey*. These long, storytelling poems are still famous today.

Each city-state had its own government. Some had kings in charge. Others were organized differently. Athens was a powerful city-state ruled by the people. The citizens chose their leaders. They voted on laws. This was the world's first **democracy**.

In Athens, only free adult men were called citizens. They took part in the government. Each year, 500 were chosen to run the day-to-day business of the city.

Pericles (*center*) was a powerful leader in Athens who helped shape democracy.

Games and Gods

People from the different city-states came together to trade and celebrate. Beginning in 776 BCE, ancient Greeks began meeting for the Olympic Games. Every four years, they would compete in sporting events.

The Games were meant to celebrate the Greek god Zeus. He was the king of the gods in Greek **mythology**.

The modern Olympics started again in 1896. The first modern Games took place in Athens. This was in honor of their Greek beginnings. Today, the Olympics take place in different countries every two years.

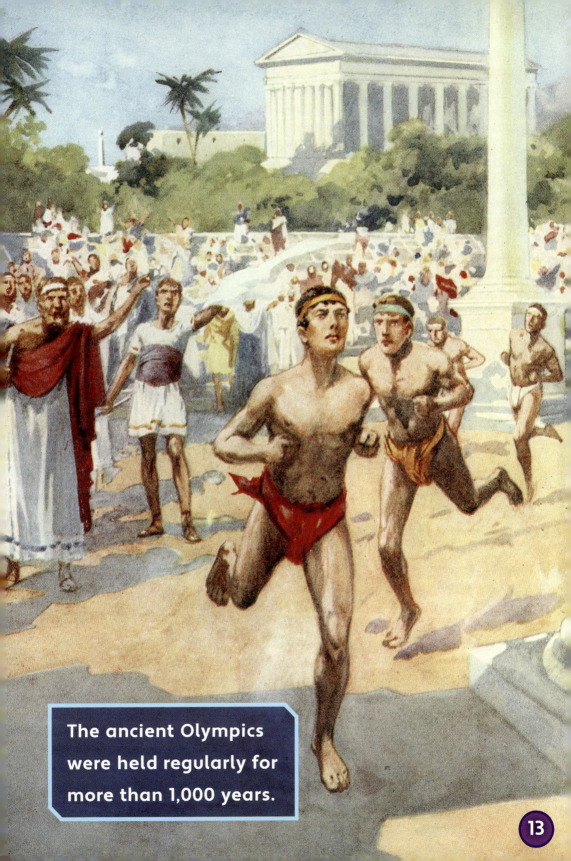

The ancient Olympics were held regularly for more than 1,000 years.

Spreading Out

Greek city-states grew. Soon, the ancient Greeks needed more space. City-states sent their people to other lands. These new Greek **colonies** were often full of new **resources**. They became an important source of trade. Some colonies even grew large enough to become their own city-states.

The ancient Greeks had colonies in Europe, Asia, and Africa. They spread ancient Greek culture wherever they went.

Corcyra was an early Greek colony.

Successes and Struggles

The Archaic period was followed by the Classical period. This era ran from about 480 to 323 BCE.

Ancient Greeks of this time made strides in science and math. Philosophers Socrates, Plato, and Aristotle became famous. Theater was very popular.

In 387 BCE, Plato formed a school. It was called the Academy. This was a place where many great thinkers gathered. They taught philosophy, math, biology, and **astronomy**.

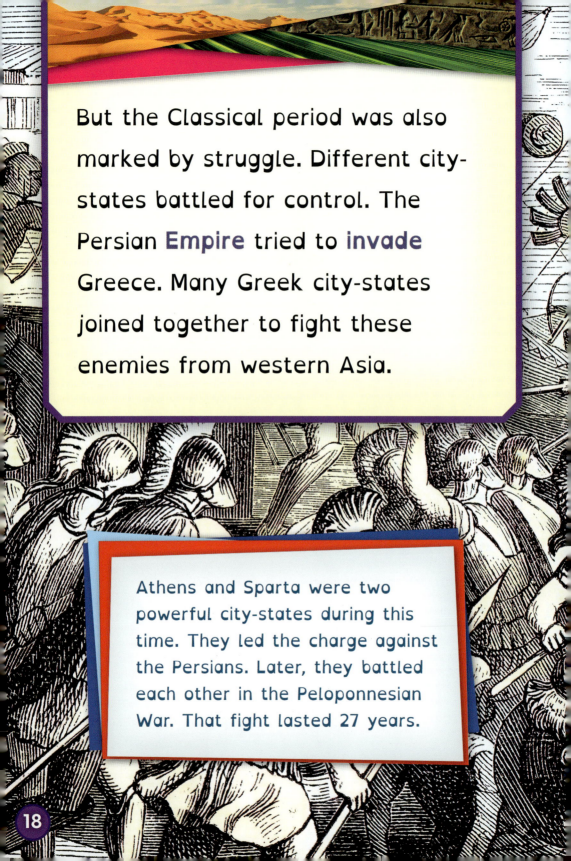

But the Classical period was also marked by struggle. Different city-states battled for control. The Persian Empire tried to invade Greece. Many Greek city-states joined together to fight these enemies from western Asia.

Athens and Sparta were two powerful city-states during this time. They led the charge against the Persians. Later, they battled each other in the Peloponnesian War. That fight lasted 27 years.

A battle in the Peloponnesian War

A Great King

In 338 BCE, King Philip II of Macedon (MAS-si-duhn) invaded. He became the ruler of all of ancient Greece. Philip II was killed in 336 BCE. His son, Alexander the Great, took over.

Alexander grew the Greek empire. It came to include parts of modern-day Asia and Africa.

In 332 BCE, Alexander the Great took over parts of Egypt. He set up the city of Alexandria and made it Egypt's capital.

Alexander the Great

An End to It All

With Alexander the Great's death in 323 BCE, the ancient Greek empire started to come to an end. The Greeks entered the Hellenistic period. This would be the final era of the once-powerful civilization. As Greece was struggling, a new civilization was rising to power.

After Alexander the Great died, his empire was broken into smaller kingdoms. These smaller kingdoms started fighting one another for control.

Alexander the Great's death

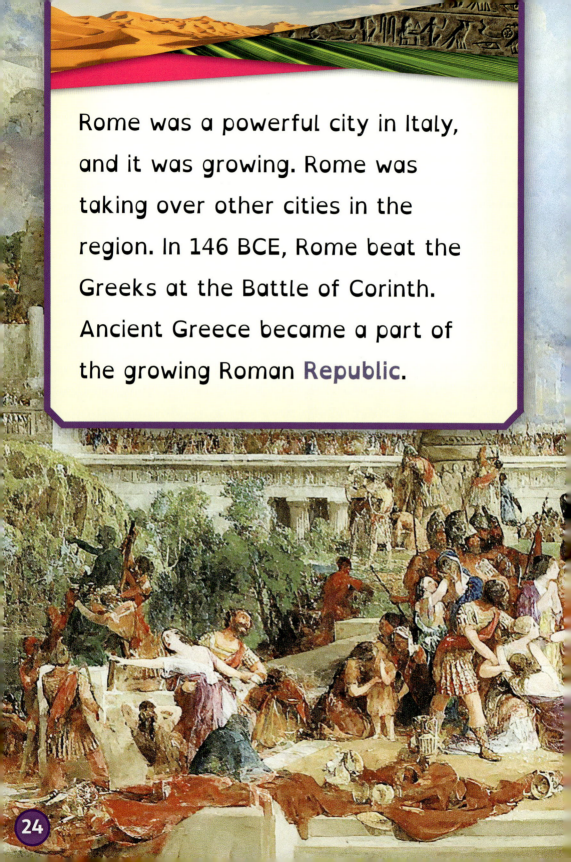

Rome was a powerful city in Italy, and it was growing. Rome was taking over other cities in the region. In 146 BCE, Rome beat the Greeks at the Battle of Corinth. Ancient Greece became a part of the growing Roman **Republic**.

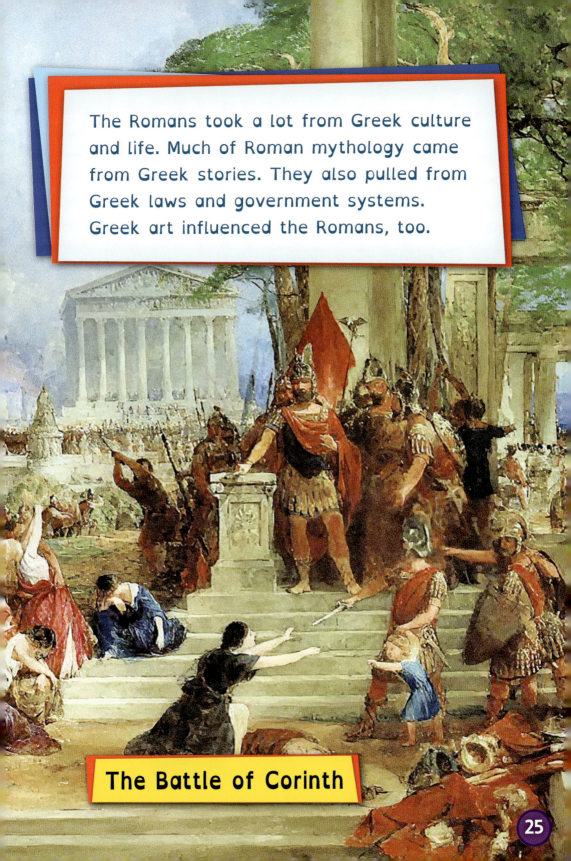

The Romans took a lot from Greek culture and life. Much of Roman mythology came from Greek stories. They also pulled from Greek laws and government systems. Greek art influenced the Romans, too.

The Battle of Corinth

Gone but Not Forgotten

The ancient Greek civilization ended more than 2,000 years ago. But we still see its ideas in modern politics. Today's art pulls from the works of the Greeks long ago. This civilization laid the groundwork for our earliest understandings of science. Though it is gone, ancient Greece is not forgotten.

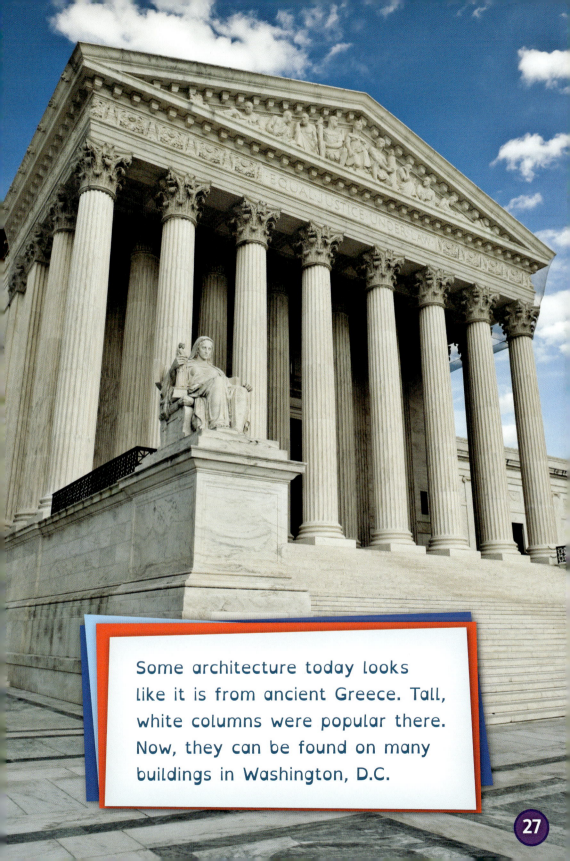

Some architecture today looks like it is from ancient Greece. Tall, white columns were popular there. Now, they can be found on many buildings in Washington, D.C.

Ancient Greece Timeline

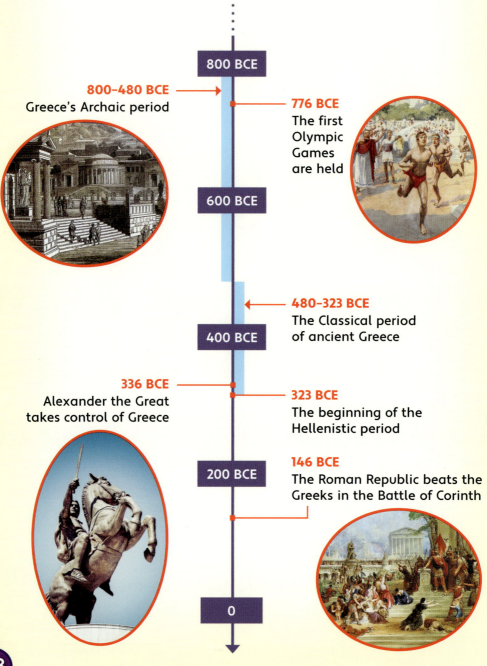

800 BCE

800–480 BCE
Greece's Archaic period

776 BCE
The first Olympic Games are held

600 BCE

480–323 BCE
The Classical period of ancient Greece

400 BCE

336 BCE
Alexander the Great takes control of Greece

323 BCE
The beginning of the Hellenistic period

146 BCE
The Roman Republic beats the Greeks in the Battle of Corinth

200 BCE

0

SilverTips for SUCCESS

★ SilverTips for REVIEW

Review what you've learned. Use the text to help you.

Define key terms

Alexander the Great
Archaic period
city-states
Classical period
Hellenistic period

Check for understanding

What was the role of the city-state in the formation of ancient Greece?

Name the three periods of ancient Greek history and describe an important event from each.

What led to the fall of ancient Greek civilization?

Think deeper

In what ways has the world of ancient Greece impacted your life today?

★ SilverTips on TEST-TAKING

- **Make a study plan.** Ask your teacher what the test is going to cover. Then, set aside time to study a little bit every day.

- **Read all the questions carefully.** Be sure you know what is being asked.

- **Skip any questions** you don't know how to answer right away. Mark them and come back later if you have time.

Glossary

astronomy the study of outer space

civilization a large group of people who share the same history and way of life

colonies areas that have been settled by people from another country and are ruled by that country

democracy a form of government in which people chose leaders by voting

empire a large region ruled by a single person or government

invade to take over a place by force

mythology a collection of stories told by people to explain beliefs or natural events

philosophy the study of ideas about the meaning of life

republic a government and society where power belongs to the people who make choices by voting

resources materials, often found in nature, that are useful or valuable

Read More

Mather, Charis. *The Peculiar Past in Ancient Greece (Strange History).* Minneapolis: Bearport Publishing Company, 2024.

Quick, Megan. *How Did Kids Live in Ancient Greece? (Kids in History).* Buffalo, NY: Gareth Stevens Publishing, 2024.

Reynolds, Donna. *Ancient Greece Revealed (Unearthing Ancient Civilizations).* New York: Cavendish Square Publishing, 2023.

Learn More Online

1. Go to **www.factsurfer.com** or scan the QR code below.
2. Enter "**Civilizations Ancient Greece**" into the search box.
3. Click on the cover of this book to see a list of websites.

Index

Aegean Sea 6–7

Alexander the Great 20–23, 28

Archaic period 8, 16, 28

Athens 10–12, 18

city-states 8, 10, 12, 14, 18

Classical period 16, 18, 28

colonies 14–15

democracy 10–11

Hellenistic period 22, 28

mythology 12, 25

Olympic Games 12–13, 28

Persian Empire 18

Philip II, King 20

philosophers 16

Rome 24

Sparta 18

About the Author

D. R. Faust is a freelance writer of fiction and nonfiction. They live in Queens, NY.